LITTLE
BIG
SOFTWARE
IDEAS

Brandon
Pearman

TOPICS

ABOUT

This book is made up of short ideas, which means there is little explanation to them. Therefore it is up to you to question them further or ignore them, to take them at face value or understand the deeper meaning.

Each idea in this book falls into one these categories:

Conventional ideas
You will probably agree with a lot of these

Controversial ideas
You will probably disagree with a lot of these

Obvious ideas
You will probably wonder why I even mention these

Mad ideas
Again you will probably wonder why I even mention these

The views expressed here are mine alone and do not reflect the view of any employers.

GOAL

In this book I hope to remind you of some core software development ideas and to challenge you to think about other ideas. Some of these ideas may conflict with what you currently believe but an experimental mindset may open new avenues for you, but just remember that...

THERE ARE MANY WAYS TO WRITE SOFTWARE AND I'M NOT SAYING YOUR WAY IS WRONG.

Little Big Software Ideas - Brandon Pearman

THANKS TO THE REVIEWERS:

- Nicolaas Strecker
- Xhanti Bomela
- Daniel Eferemo
- Sulungeka Roundy Faltein
- Hugo Monsembula Ibuo
- Andrew Dott
- Dhiren Appalraju

There were quite a few debates regarding some of these pages. What we often found is that it is important to consider nuance, context and circumstance.

Some people/companies have different processes/policies and use terms differently to others. I cant consider everything when making general statements. Therefore it is up to you to figure out how these ideas could be applied.

Lastly, thanks to my wife Kameshini for all her support throughout my career.

COMMUNICATION

Jargon and acronyms may make someone sound smart,

but it makes them a bad communicator

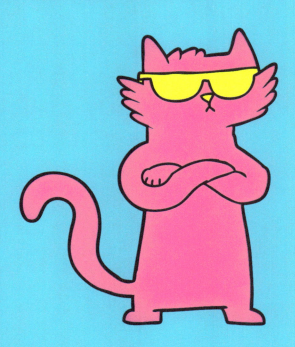

Not asking for clarity on jargon or acronyms keeps someone from looking dumb,

but it makes them a bad communicator

Absolutes are not agile

"never"   "always"

"right"   "wrong"

"This will never change"

Absolutes instill a rigid mindset and probably lead to more rigid designs.

Absolutes communicate that "there are no possible alternatives".
Maybe a particular solution "will ALWAYS work", but stating that means you don't do any further thinking on the topic to confirm that.

Little Big Software Ideas - Brandon Pearman

The language we use has strong influences on decisions

"best practice"

"hacky"

Its best practice because its best practice

"pattern"

"anti-pattern"

Labeling solutions with buzzwords often influences decisions despite any real backing.

Be wary of solutions that are nothing but buzzwords. Make sure to understand how it actually solves your particular problem.

Keep the focus on the merits of the solution.

Some things are impossible until you believe it is possible

Shutting down someone's idea by saying it's impossible, means the possibilities will not be explored.

First ask yourself, how would it work if it were possible?

Little Big Software Ideas - Brandon Pearman

If you can't say why something "should" or "shouldn't" be

then don't use the word "should"

Code **should** be written this way because I say so

According to who? The word "should" is often used as a way of asserting some universal authority over the topic, but has no real backing on its own. Make sure it is followed up by reasoning.

Back up why it "should"

Code is not just instructions to a computer, it is also communication with your fellow developers and your future self.

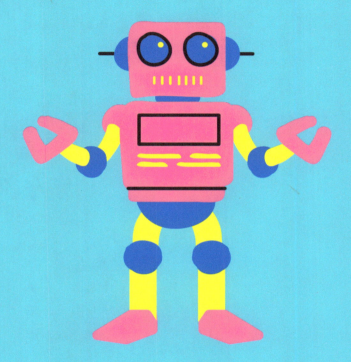

We don't write 1's and 0's because code is meant to be read by humans

Appealing to authority is the weakest argument even though it feels like a strong one

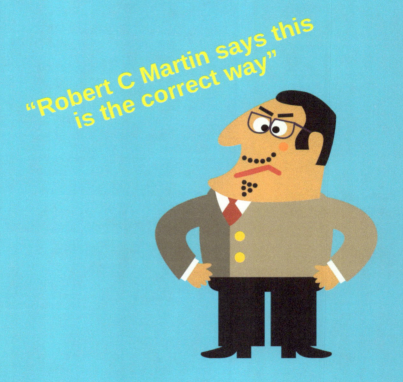

"Robert C Martin says this is the correct way"

If all experts agree on the same point, then appealing to authority may be valid, but in software development you will look far and wide to find something that all experts agree on.

Little Big Software Ideas - Brandon Pearman

Many issues stem from overlooking the obvious

We generally make assumptions about the obvious, and assumptions lead to mistakes. Therefore question the obvious and double check that everyone has the same interpretation. What is obvious to you is not obvious to everyone else.

Little Big Software Ideas - Brandon Pearman

Good communicators do more than speak well

Good communicators excel at eliciting clear thoughts from others through effective questioning.

Good communicators clarify the thoughts of others to gain a deeper understanding.

ie Asking the right questions can greatly improve communication.

Little Big Software Ideas - Brandon Pearman

Clearly expressing your ideas not only helps others comprehend them,

but also helps you gain a clearer and deeper understanding

When thinking about the clearest way to explain something, you may find yourself exploring different avenues of the idea, kind of like rubber duck debugging

Little Big Software Ideas - Brandon Pearman

DESIGN

Check your design bias

The common phrase "It depends", has an obvious flaw, and that is the designer's bias. Developers tend to choose the design they personally prefer or have lots of experience with, over the most efficient. That's often fine because a developer will do better with designs they have more knowledge and experience in.

But it's dishonest to say that "It depends" and then choose based on your personal bias. Rather say "This option is better because we know it, and cannot afford the learning curve of a new design". Understanding your bias will help improve your design skills.

If you get told "it depends" you need to find out what it depends on and what the alternatives are.

"It depends"

Does it?

On what?

Sometimes a problem doesn't need a solution

it needs to not exist at all

Before attempting to solve a problem, first check if changing the existing design will eliminate the problem.

Pattern Driven Development is when someone writes code based on a set of patterns, rather than basing it on fit.

It is common for someone to love a specific:
-pattern
-architecture
-technology
-package

and then they use it for everything

eg always use CQRS, ES, Microservices, DDD or decorator pattern for every problem.

Pattern Driven Development is when someone comes up with a solution first... then applies it to their problems.

PDD is clearly used when every problem at the company/team is solved the same way.

Sometimes a decision comes down to which issues you can live with

Mathematics is easy because most problems have an answer.

Software development is difficult because we often have to choose between several bad answers.

You are responsible for your dependencies

Your customer/stakeholder doesn't care that you didn't write the code in the dependency when their application is exposed to downtime, bugs, security risks or is too difficult to extend.

Little Big Software Ideas - Brandon Pearman

Code repetition is not evil, repetitive representation is

If two functions have duplicate code but represent different knowledge, then separating them will allow them to evolve on their own, without them being coupled to each other.

DRY code is coupled code

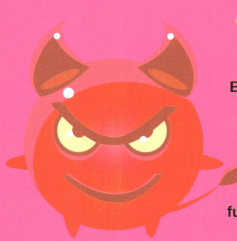

Eg two services may perform vastly different functions but have some similar code. Sharing that "duplicated" code will couple two functions which have nothing to do with each other.

Building your own framework is not easy

If you choose to build a framework, so that the many teams at your company can use it:

You need to think about and build every possible solution that every team would need, else risk blocking them.

You need to make sure the interfaces are clear in purpose but are general enough to be used for many cases, else risk confusion on what to use.

You need to keep the bugs out, else risk causing issues everywhere at the same time.

You need to keep documentation good, else risk delaying teams trying to figure out how to use it.

Bottom Line: probably a bad idea

Little Big Software Ideas - Brandon Pearman

Knowledge
"I don't know how it works, it's magic"

Responsibility
"I'm waiting for the architect to fix an issue"

Autonomy
"We can't change that, it's how the framework works"

Productivity
"The framework does not support what we need"

Innovation
"The framework forces one way, and we can't try anything different"

Developer happiness
"The framework is getting in the way"

Frameworks can have serious negative impacts on a team

Little Big Software Ideas - Brandon Pearman

26

Today's best practices have become best practice, after someone broke the best practices of their time

Experimental ideas can backfire or it can produce untold rewards. Know when to experiment and when to not.

Rules are in place because they are correct most of the time, masters of a craft know when the rules do NOT apply.

Little Big Software Ideas - Brandon Pearman

Interpretation of best practices, creates a range of "best practices"

For Example, How you apply the single responsibility principle depends on how you define a responsibility.

While you think you understand what the original author of a best practice was meaning, so does the next person. To find common ground sometimes we need to be flexible in our understanding of best practices.

Before you refactor "poor" code
first try to understand the original reasoning

Sometimes code is bad for a reason, and changing it will have unforeseen consequences. Understanding the original intent will greatly improve your redesign decisions.

You can try to find the original reasoning in documentation or by speaking to the original developers, else try to put yourself in their shoes, and try to think of possible reasons (then realize you need to document your design decisions for the next person).

Little Big Software Ideas - Brandon Pearman

Strict designs can damage a system

Designs that have no room for deviation, don't allow developers to adapt to the specific problems at coding time.

By NOT specifying implementation details, the design will be more broad and flexible, allowing developers to create the best solution as needs reveal themselves at code time.

CV Driven Development

Pattern Driven Development

Cargo cult programming

Define your system requirements

Then plugin tech which meets those requirements

Are you building your system around the chosen tech or selecting the tech which fits your needs?

If your system is highly coupled and dependent on a given tech then more than likely the system is built around the tech.

Design your system without any tech, then find tech which fits your design.

Design for
human error

BAD Code

and don't assume something will always work

BAD Deploy

BAD Infrastructure

BAD Data

BAD Design

Assume mistakes will get made and prepare for them.
- Cordoned off deploys and security
- Validation and Verification
- Monitoring and logs
- Rollback strategies
- Error handling
- Tests

But most importantly

while designing and coding, always ask "what if this fails in some unforeseen manner?"

I have never worked on a significant system without mistakes being made.

COLLABORATIVE PROGRAMMING

You don't have to always do pair programming

Pick the correct style for the job. Different tasks may require different approaches, it may be solo, pair or mob programming. As you pick up a task, determine what will work best for it.

Not everybody on the team has to do pair programming

The team doesn't have to have a mandate to force pair programming. It is ok if some devs work more in pairs and others work more solo.

"Individuals and interactions over processes and tools"
-agilemanifesto https://agilemanifesto.org/

Little Big Software Ideas - Brandon Pearman

35

It is very easy for a more dominant personality or a more senior developer to take over the direction of a pair programming session. That person should do their best to involve the other person, ask questions and listen to their ideas.

If someone is overpowering you all the time, and not attempting to collaborate with you, try prompting more dialogue with them else avoid programming with them.

Always hear your partner out

The limiting factor when working with complex solutions is the mind... not the fingers

More minds on a complex task will generally produce better solutions with less bugs in better time.

At first pair programming sounds like a bad idea.
You may feel that it
will reduce the control and ownership of what you write,
or that the other person will just get in your way,
or it will just be a waste of time.

But when developers try it,
often they find the exact opposite.

Most devs think pair programming is a bad idea
until they give it a fair go

Little Big Software Ideas - Brandon Pearman

Feedback at coding time

is better than feedback at code review time

Feedback at coding time is a faster feedback loop which contributes to better solutions completed faster. But it also solves another common issue

When a dev has invested time and effort into their code, they may feel a little attached to it, and not react well when someone tears it apart.
It is easier to have discussions at coding time where the dev is still thinking about possible solutions, and is open to brainstorming ideas together.

Little Big Software Ideas - Brandon Pearman

39

Pair programming helps team members align with each other

When devs discuss solutions on a regular basis, they start to understand how one another thinks and they find common ground. This is very valuable if you need a well aligned, in sync team.

Pair programming can save time with

less code reviews, less bugs & less refactorings

Since a second person has looked at the code while coding, the need for code reviews declines. Since two people have thought of the best possible solution, there is a lower chance of bugs or a need for big refactorings.

Little Big Software Ideas - Brandon Pearman

Pair programming has built in knowledge sharing

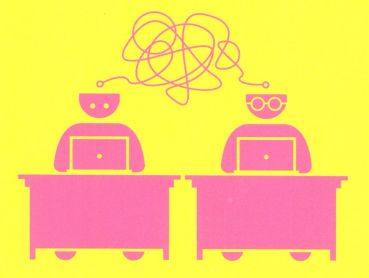

Having only one dev know how a particular piece of code works is risky. Often when one dev is an expert in an area, they will continue to work in that area, which only leads to a greater knowledge gap in the team, and a greater dependency on that dev. Pairs allow more than one dev to understand different areas of the code base.

It is more likely for an issue to be missed in a code review, than in pair programming

You may think that you still need code reviews because a pair can miss something. Sure they can, but so can code reviewers. In fact it is far easier for a pair to detect issues, than it is for a code reviewer.

Obvious Caveat: If it's a Junior pair, then having a senior do a code review may still be necessary.

Informally choose how you pair program

The common advice on how to pair is to have one person type and the other solution. This is one pairing style.

You don't have to have a formal method to get value from pairing. Simply try different things and change up regularly.

eg both code via a shared IDE or both solution then code

Little Big Software Ideas - Brandon Pearman

TESTING

Unit tests will only test what you tell them to test

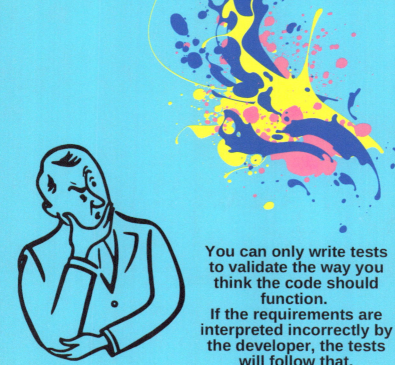

You can only write tests to validate the way you think the code should function.
If the requirements are interpreted incorrectly by the developer, the tests will follow that.

tests are fallible

Little Big Software Ideas - Brandon Pearman

46

Unit tests shine at giving confidence to refactor

Unit tests will make sure the code works the same before and after a refactoring.

Unit tests can be a type of documentation

if you write them as such

To do this, try keep your tests inline with what you expect the application to do

Organize your tests in a logical manner that makes it easy for someone to understand a particular feature and its functions

Just because you are writing unit tests does not mean you are doing TDD.

Unit tests != TDD

TDD is a workflow, where unit tests are written before the code. Then as the code is completed it can be verified against the expectations setup by the tests.

TDD works better for some people/problems more than others.

Little Big Software Ideas - Brandon Pearman

Code coverage does not mean your code is tested
it means it is covered

tests are fallible

A test could cover code but do a poor job of evaluating it. ie Code coverage does not quantify the quality of your tests.

Tests which are difficult to understand, are just as bad as code which is difficult to understand

Consider the complexity of your tests, and try to simplify them the same way you would simplify any other code.

Your tests may be complex because they are neglected or over engineered,
OR
your tests may be complex because the code it is testing is also complex or over engineered.

Code quality checkers will keep a consistent style and catch some basic issues but it wont prevent bugs.

Code checkers should be used for the sake of the devs, but can be counter productive if it managed by people outside the team. Therefore the devs should control their own code checkers.

Automated code quality checkers do not catch bugs

Unit testing can be a design tool

If your business logic needs to be decoupled from:

infrastructure

frameworks

web

database dependencies

clients

then making your code unit testable, also means you have to design your code in this flexible manner.

Tool not a rule

LAW

If someone can make bug inducing changes to the code base, but the tests still pass, then the test quality is poor.

To gauge test quality

consider what changes in the code base, will fail the tests

Don't get too caught up in the exact definitions of test types

What exactly is a unit test?

What is an integration test?

Component test?

Perf test?

End to end test?

Contract test?

Stress test?

I like unit tests but some great engineers which I respect prefer mostly end to end tests.
(we debate this a lot)

Bottom line is, if your tests are stable, maintainable, and give you confidence then that's fine.
If your tests work for you, then you do not need to force your testing to conform with some industry norms like test pyramid, full isolation, test first, etc.

Little Big Software Ideas - Brandon Pearman

Maintainable tests don't change when the system under test changes

One way to do this is to test the results of your functionality, and not the implementation details. Your tests need to be as unaware of your code as possible.

COMPLEXITY

The core cause of complexity is cognitive overload

Cognitive overload is when you can't keep track of everything, because there are too many dependencies, patterns, layers, states, conditions, cases, branches, classes, etc.

Little Big Software Ideas - Brandon Pearman

Short code is not necessarily
simple code

Refactoring 4 lines of code into 1 line may make it more complex. A monstrous 1 liner can be harder to read and debug.

Measurable complexity erroneously gets more attention than non-measurable complexity

We can easily measure lines of code, cyclomatic complexity, code duplication, coupling, etc; therefore these generally get more attention.

It's harder to measure readability, understandability, maintainability, and discoverability; therefore these often get less attention.

An overly complex solution makes a company reliant on the expert that created it

This means that overly complex solutions are bad for the company and it's developers but good for the contractor/architect/speaker/saas owner/package owner

Tech advice and patterns are sometimes just a sales tactic?

Be aware of advice when the expert giving the advice sells a product or a service. Often an expert would sell a certain pattern as the cure for everything, but then it leads to dependency on their product or service to make it work well.
eg someone doing consultations, talks and courses promoting a highly complex event driven architecture which sells a library to manage events.

This doesn't mean these experts don't share any valuable ideas, it just means be aware of their ulterior motive and navigate around it. ie be aware of vender lock in and coupling

Decisions are irreversible when it's too expensive to change

For example, it may be too difficult to change your applications programming language, database, or some critical pattern. You could say those are irreversible decisions. When you initillay decide on these, think long and hard about them.

Leaky abstractions may lead to the underlying implementation becoming "irreversible" over time

You can identify a leak by considering what it would take to replace the implementation.
If changes in the abstracted implementation lead to changes in the caller, then you have a leak.

You may have created an abstraction to have the ability to change an implementation in the future, but if that abstraction is leaking too many details of its implementation, then it may become too expensive to change.
You have to double down on your abstraction and make it airtight or consider removing the abstraction because it has lost its usefulness.

Little Big Software Ideas - Brandon Pearman

64

Too many irreversible decisions will eventually corner you.

When existing patterns are inflexible and can not accommodate a new feature, then devs have to work around it, which adds to the complexity.

Work arounds mean an additional concept is needed

Work arounds are usually where "hacky" code comes from

Little Big Software Ideas - Brandon Pearman

Coupling the bulk of your logic or boundaries to an implementation may lead to the underlying implementation becoming "irreversible" over time.

For example if your microservices communicate via some queue technology, it may be too expensive to change that queue technology. Or if your core logic is built around some pattern like CQRS or actors it may be too expensive to change that.

This is not necessarily bad, just be aware of that these are therefore important decisions.

A single change may not be complex, but when summed up with many such changes it may cause complexity

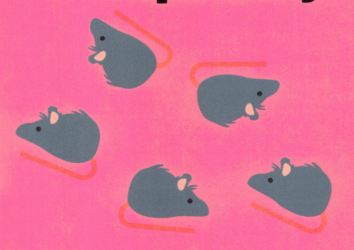

For example one "if" statement is not complex but over time when a thousand are added up, you end up with a complex system. Each change is so small you don't notice the growing complexity.

Is 1 class with 1000 lines worse than 1000 classes with 1 line each?

You don't have to choose either, there is a middle ground.

There is no one size fits all rule on how small or large your classes/methods should be.
Do what works best for each situation.

Note: principles are NOT rules.

Too many dependencies add to
complexity

If you don't need that database, queue, class, package, API, etc. then don't use it.

If you need it later, then add it later.

YAGNI

Junior devs write simple code because they
dont know better

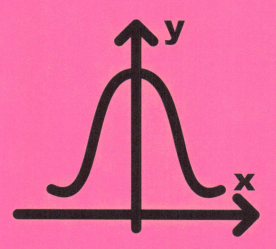

Senior devs write simple code because they
know better

Devs often reach a point in their career where they learn about design patterns and want to use it everywhere. This leads to over engineering.

Senior devs tend to not be pattern obsessed, but instead orientated to find specific solutions.

Documentation should not be used to cover up bad code

Documentation:

is usually out of date

takes more time to write

can be just as unreadable as the code

may be hard for others to find

but most of all it does nothing to improve a bad code base.

AGILE

Agile is not a management style
it is the ability to change rapidly

Strict rules reduce agility.
True agility requires flexibility and an open mind.
Therefore agile is shapeless.

"Be formless, shapeless, like water.
You put water into a cup, it becomes the cup.
You put water into a bottle, it becomes the bottle.
You put it into a teapot, it becomes the teapot.
Now water can flow or it can crash.
Be water, my friend." - Bruce Lee

Little Big Software Ideas - Brandon Pearman

Smaller delivery means you deliver sooner.

Delivering sooner means
you get feedback sooner.

Getting feedback sooner means
you can change direction sooner.

What is a deliverable?

A complete ticket, a deploy, a release, working user functionality or something else?

How small is small?

1 days work, or 2, 5, 10, 20, 40 days' work?

Who is giving you feedback?

Another dev, or someone in business, or the product's customer?

Do these answers have to apply universally or can they change as needed?

Agile does not force every delivery to be as "small" as you think

"Deliver working software frequently, from a couple of weeks to a couple of months, with a preference to the shorter timescale."
-agilemanifesto
https://agilemanifesto.org/principles.html

is "a couple of months" small?

From a business perspective is there value in a ticket so small that it does not produce a viable piece of functionality, which means you can't get business feedback on it?

Is there value in breaking up work simply to fit into arbitrary timeframes or sizes?

Does breaking up the work, always make estimates more accurate?
eg if you break a 3 point story into 10 stories.

Little Big Software Ideas - Brandon Pearman

Measure a team's success by

the satisfaction of the users, product owners and stakeholders

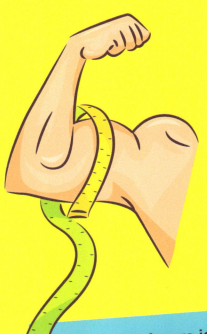

Measuring a team by story points, velocity, charts, lines of code, or bugs is poor practice because output is not the same as outcome.

A team that completes many story points but produces no working software, is inferior to a team that does very little story points but produces working software that the end user loves.

"Working software is the primary measure of progress."
- agilemanifesto
https://agilemanifesto.org/principles.html

Little Big Software Ideas - Brandon Pearman

Being agile allows you to
Adapt as needed

For example, if cutting your deployments down from every 6 months to every 2 weeks makes you more agile, then deploying when you need makes you even more agile. You could say the same for other processes like planning, review and retrospectives. ie ceremonies as needed is more agile than forced timeframes.

Little Big Software Ideas - Brandon Pearman

Not allowing change
is NOT agile

Defining a strict rigid process with rules that cannot change is not agile. Could you change the way you do sprints, estimates, meetings, or code within a reasonable timeframe. If no, then you are not agile.

"Mandatory agile" is not agile.

The time it takes to change something is the best indicator of your agility

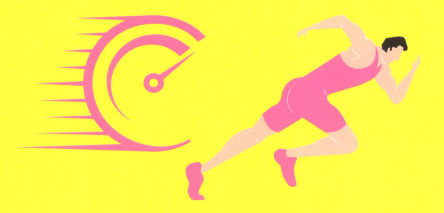

A company may be able to change something but if it takes them months or years to do so then they are still not agile. Change could be features, processes, technology, tools, people, etc

You can be agile without estimates or ceremonies

How?

1. Don't force the same tools or processes on everyone. Let teams organize themselves.

2. Focus on incremental working software.

3. Focus on communication and involving everyone in discussions.

4. Be open to changing anything anytime, and write code that can do that.

5. Add as many feedback loops as possible

Caveats:
1. Mature senior devs are required
2. The company needs to be able to trust their senior devs

Committing to an exact estimate is not agile, nor is it honest

Beside the fact that the agile manifesto makes no mention of estimating, it is common practice in "agile" teams...

Often estimates are treated as deadlines because managers / scrum masters force developers to commit to an amount of work within a given timeframe eg 10sp in a sprint.

Developers know they can not give an accurate estimate all the time. The most honest thing a developer can do is give a range.
eg 3-5sp, or 3-6days

If a single number is required then it should be treated as a deadline and use the highest possible number.

Little Big Software Ideas - Brandon Pearman

Collaboration leads to converging ideas

Good?

Bad?

Getting everyone on the same page is usually a good thing, but not always...

Some roles may require a temporary departure in thinking, such as Testers, Security or Researchers. During exploration it is better if they are not influenced by the original ideas. They can then collaborate with the team on their findings.

Little Big Software Ideas - Brandon Pearman

A development team shouldn't simply write business requirements as code, but rather

translate business requirements into a viable software solution

Collaboration

It is the development team's responsibility to understand the requirements and guide the business accordingly. By collaborating with different experts you can fully understand the problem and they can fully understand the product you are building. Developers have a strong understanding of software and can guide business to better ways of doing the same thing.

Little Big Software Ideas - Brandon Pearman

"Business people and developers must work together daily throughout the project."- agilemanifesto
https://agilemanifesto.org/principles.html

Collaboration

Your customers/business stakeholders do not always know exactly what they want

So be ready to change the code and don't expect perfect descriptions of the requirements upfront.

The best way to handle this is to work with business people daily, instead of every 2 weeks.

Little Big Software Ideas - Brandon Pearman

It is poor practice to compare teams to one another

Why?

Story points, velocity, charts, lines of code, bug count are metrics you can look at, but are not comparable between teams or individuals. Each team/individual has a unique set of circumstances, they have different skill sets, code bases, objectives, tasks and requirements.

Software development is NOT a factory line.

Factory lines produce the same product over and over again. In software development we are constantly creating new functionality, and have to deal with new problems regularly.

Little Big Software Ideas - Brandon Pearman

86

Even within a rigid "agile" framework

a development team or individual can practice agility

This is true because agility is not about sprints, stands ups and SMs. If a company has rigid policies in place, you can still improve your agility in your own working time. You don't need permission to improve your feedback loops.

How?
Read this whole chapter

Little Big Software Ideas - Brandon Pearman

If someone's job is dependent on the team doing a certain process or framework, then why would that person be open to any change in that process or framework?

How can a team be self organized when it's someone's role to organize them

Little Big Software Ideas - Brandon Pearman

Happy developers are far more productive

Not all developers are the same nor do they want the same things. A good way to manage this, is to give teams and individuals the space to create their own environment, instead of forcing them to abide to a large batch of blanket rules.

"Build projects around motivated individuals. Give them the environment and support they need, and trust them to get the job done." - agilemanifesto
https://agilemanifesto.org/principles.html

Little Big Software Ideas - Brandon Pearman

Set goals not rules
Set what you want,
not how you want it

Companies which have a high quantity of rules, and forces everyone to do everything the exact same way, tend to lose innovative and self organizing developers. This then perpetuates the need for rules and force. Give teams the goal so that they can solve the problems in their specific case. This will help cultivate and attract talent which solves problems.

"Build projects around motivated individuals. Give them the environment and support they need, and trust them to get the job done." - agilemanifesto https://agilemanifesto.org/principles.html

Agility is a scale, not an absolute

It is not as simple as being agile or not. Everything you do will make you more or less agile, leaving you somewhere in between.

ie you could be more agile than one team but less than another, even though they are all using so called agile "frameworks".

Little Big Software Ideas - Brandon Pearman

91

scrum != agile

Thinking you are agile because you do scrum, is like thinking you are as agile as a monkey because you eat bananas.

For many, Scrum has become a cargo cult.

AGILE DESIGN

Refactoring is CORE to agile code

If you include refactoring as part of every task, then there is no pressure to get designs perfect upfront.

If refactoring is a separate task then you may find it difficult to get the time to do it.

MVPs, POCs or small chunks of work

are great ways of getting started instead of big upfront designs and documentation

You know more after implementing and running code, therefore that's the safer time to make decisions.
A small boat can turn faster than a large ship. Smaller units of work allows pivoting or scraping work sooner.

Note: this small unit of work should still be viable, ie it can be used in some way

"Working software over comprehensive documentation"
- agilemanifesto https://agilemanifesto.org/

It is a great skill to know when to take action and when to plan.

You do not always have to have the "perfect" solution upfront... but sometimes you do

Difficult to reverse = more planning

Easy to reverse = more action

Little Big Software Ideas - Brandon Pearman

If a decision is difficult to correct or a failure will have a high impact, then make sure you cover as many edge cases as possible and test thoroughly.
Being cautious prevents loss of time and money caused by issues, but takes more time to get off the ground.

If you know a decision is difficult to reverse, then be damn sure about it

Last Responsible Moment

Little Big Software Ideas - Brandon Pearman

If you know a decision is easy to reverse, then action has more value than planning

If a decision is easy to correct or failure has little impact, then don't waste time deliberating and covering every edge case, just do it and be able to do corrections along the way.

Being fast allows you to learn faster and adapt to the needs of the customers, instead of the perfect plan to build the wrong product.

"If you're good at course correcting, being wrong may be less costly than you think."
-Jeff Bezos

Little Big Software Ideas - Brandon Pearman

Agile code is not necessarily maintainable code

Agile code could be patterns which make changing the implementation easy

or it could be non-invasive simple code that could easily be deleted or refactored later

caveat: Refactoring culture required

When dealing with uncertainty and small amounts of code, prefer agile code over maintainable code

Agile code is more important because you may NOT want to maintain the code, if you realize it's incorrect. If it is correct then you can spend the time to improve it.

Spending the time designing and coding something, which just gets thrown away or drastically changed is a waste.

caveat: Refactoring culture required

Little Big Software Ideas - Brandon Pearman

Not all developers agree with each other, and they don't need to

You will look far and wide to find something that all developers agree on.
If you have separate teams with their own code bases, then all devs don't have to agree with one another, only devs within the same team need to agree. This means that teams can have high autonomy, but individuals within a team must align with each other.

"The best architectures, requirements, and designs emerge from self-organizing teams."
- agilemanifesto
https://agilemanifesto.org/principles.html

Little Big Software Ideas - Brandon Pearman

Sometimes you can design pivot points between seemingly different designs

If you can't decide which solution is best, try to find or create similarities between them and start writing that. The correct path may become more clear as you go.

Order development based on expected learnings

Look at your task and choose a strategy:

Start with the areas of greater uncertainty to give more time to resolve potential issues which may arise.

Consider if tasks are unrelated

Complete simple stuff first, to increase clarity in the more complex stuff.

Consider if tasks are related

Adapt designs to your needs

There are NO perfect designs.
You need to adopt existing design patterns and then adapt it to your needs, because every team has a different set of circumstances.
This adaption takes some experimentation to find what works best.

Do not become too dogmatic about following a popular pattern exactly.

Dogma reduces adaption.

CV Driven Development

Pattern Driven Development

Cargo cult programming

Excess 3rd party dependencies reduce agility

1. Many developers tend to leak details of 3rd party dependencies or use them directly, making it difficult to change them.

2. Some dependencies have their own dependencies and requirements, which may limit your applications ability to upgrade or deploy.

3. Use of a third party dependency means you do not have full control over the functionality, meaning its hard to change details if needed.

Little Big Software Ideas - Brandon Pearman

Find balance between idealism and pragmatism

Being too idealistic often leads to:

over engineering

analysis paralysis

cookie cutter solutions

Sometimes you have to do the best with what you have and recognize the limitations.

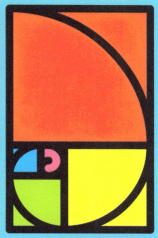

Being too pragmatic often leads to:

lack of consistent design

sloppy cowboy programming

reinventing the wheel

Sometimes you have to dream big and reach for unobtainable goals.

Think tools
Not rules

Design principles often get used as a set of rules

even though they were never intended to be one size fits all rules.

Be agile in the way you think about design.

Principles and patterns are tools, not rules, you may choose to use in your design, or not.

Little Big Software Ideas - Brandon Pearman

Occam's razor

"When faced with two possible explanations, the simpler of the two is the one most likely to be true"

Occam's engineer

When faced with two possible designs, the simpler of the two is the one most likely to be agile

but simple is often avoided because its not new and shiny enough, nor is it great for job security or CV building.

CULTURE

Culture is a collection of common behaviors between all the individuals

The feeling of culture comes when most people are doing the same things. For example, if the majority is friendly.

Therefore, every individual adds to the culture and is responsible for it.

Culture is highly influenced by leaders

A leader may not necessarily have a leadership title at the company, but is capable of leading others.

"The world is changed by your example, not by your opinion."
- Paulo Coelho

Little Big Software Ideas - Brandon Pearman

Software is directly impacted by culture

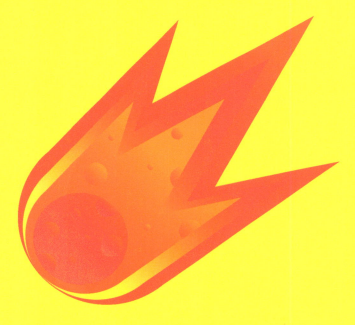

Culture forms how the devs write code and greatly impacts innovation, collaboration, participation, team work, communication, responsibility, and knowledge sharing

You can't force culture

Telling everyone to be innovative will not make them innovative.

Create opportunities for individuals to choose to take up roles and responsibilities which suit their natural beneficial qualities.

Instead of telling the team what you expect from them, tell them what they should expect from you.

Committing to actions you value will cultivate that culture over time

In the next few pages I cover my pledge to my team, which has strong mature senior developers. This is based on my circumstances at the time of writing this but I expect it to change for different teams. Even though this pledge is very situational, it will provide an example for you. Adopt what you like and add what you need. You don't need any specific title in order to commit to your values.

This is my pledge to my team, and NOT what I expect from them. Remember you can't force culture, only be what you want, and provide an example for others to choose to follow.

I commit to
not point fingers

Safe Environment

I will accept my mistakes and never blame you for them.

I will not allow others to blame you for their mistakes.

I do NOT care whose fault it is, I care about fixing the problem.

Little Big Software Ideas - Brandon Pearman

I commit to
learn from mistakes

I will treat failures as a lesson and an opportunity to grow.

Fail Safe

I will not hide my failures but instead, share the lessons with the team.

I commit to
creating a comfortable environment for others to speak up and disagree

I will support diverse ideas.

I will always listen to your ideas, thoughts, concerns, opinions.

I will not attack anyone personally or get angry over input I disagree with.

I will always protect your right to disagree with anyone on anything.

I will encourage seamingly "dumb" questions.

Diversity of ideas

Little Big Software Ideas - Brandon Pearman

I commit to
take responsibility as a team

I will help fix mistakes/issues even if I was never involved in the first place.

I will acknowledge the whole team and it's individuals for their achievements, and not steal the glory from them.

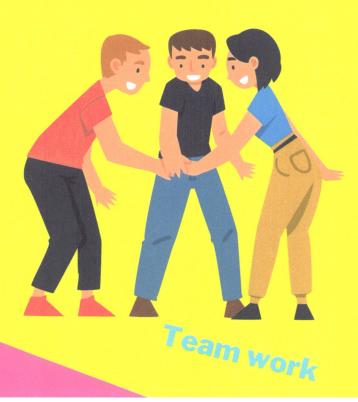

Team work

I commit to
find the best ideas

**I will always break down input
logically and not emotionally.**

**I will always give logical rational
reasoning, and not just add labels to
manipulate everyone's view
eg "best practice", "anti-pattern".**

**I will not take criticism personally
because I know that criticism of an idea
is not a criticism of me.**

**I will present ideas but will not attach
my ego to it.**

Little Big Software Ideas - Brandon Pearman

I commit to
do my best on decisions made

If consensus can not be reached, I will still commit to the decision made by the SME/leader/senior/owner.

When I disagree with the decision made, I will focus on why the decision was made and it's strengths.

When I disagree with the decision made, I will do my best to follow through with it anyway.

Little Big Software Ideas - Brandon Pearman

I commit to
give opportunities to individuals

I will involve everyone and make sure everyone has a chance to be heard.

I will invite others to participate in my work/idea/conversation.

I will provide opportunities for others to step up and take the lead.

Growth

I commit to
foster knowledge sharing

I will give opportunities for anyone to share their knowledge.

I will share my knowledge

I will review completed work with the team (functionality and code).

I will give feedback on your work, questions, etc.

I will ask for your feedback on my work.

Little Big Software Ideas - Brandon Pearman

122

I commit to
take action

I will follow up on decisions made by the team and get them implemented.

I will do my best to understand the company goals, our team goals and each individual's personal goals so that I can take action which helps to reach those goals.

I will find ways to provide value to the team.

Little Big Software Ideas - Brandon Pearman

123

I commit to
give independence to devs

I will recognize an individual's autonomy, and trust they will do what they believe is best within the bounds of the company or team alignment.

I will help enforce the boundaries of the team and of individuals, so that they have a high degree of control over their own work.

I will offer guidance and vision but not commands.

Remember: Cultivate the culture you need, for your environment

The past few pages were my pledge to my team, which has strong mature senior developers. My pledge is catered for me but will provide an example for you. Adopt what you like and add what you need.

This is my pledge to my team, and NOT what I expect from them. Remember you can't force culture, only be what you want and provide an example for others to choose to follow.

Little Big Software Ideas - Brandon Pearman

THANK YOU

I hope these ideas were able to remind you of some core software development ideas and were able to challenge you to think about other ideas.

There are many ways to write software and I hope you are inspired to experiment with some new ideas.

The views expressed here are mine alone and do not reflect the view of any employers.

Little Big Software Ideas - Brandon Pearman

www.ingramcontent.com/pod-product-compliance
Lightning Source LLC
LaVergne TN
LVHW072049060326
832903LV00053B/303